IRREGULAR WARFARE: COUNTERTERRORISM FORCES IN SUPPORT OF COUNTERINSURGENCY OPERATIONS

On October 19th, 2001, a joint special operations task force parachuted onto Objective Rhino, a remote desert landing strip southwest of Kandahar, Afghanistan.[1] This was the overt insertion of counterterrorism (CT) forces into the country.[2] For the next seven years, the CT forces operated in the shadows, protecting information about all facets of its organization and operations from US and coalition forces as vigorously and competently as it protected them from the enemies it targeted. Despite the innate culture of secrecy that permeated early CT force operations, the counterinsurgency operating environment demanded greater transparency if the CT force was to sustain effects or achieve the increased effects desired.[3] The CT force aggressively responded to the environment and dramatically and continuously increased internal and external coordination and cooperation in order to increase its freedom of action – ability to operate – and achieve sought effects. This effort will focus on unclassified actions taken by the CT force to increase its freedom of action and thus effects in two very different counterinsurgency operating environments – Afghanistan and Iraq. Generic inferences will illuminate, and ideally help preserve, the CT force efforts and lessons without compromising ongoing efforts and effects.

Counterterrorism force is a purposefully generic term that will be used throughout this paper to discuss United States Special Operations Command's (USSOCOM) counterterrorism forces. The sub-units that compose the CT force do not warrant identification in this forum and would add nothing to the narrative. It is relevant to acknowledge that as a unified command, USSOCOM is a joint headquarters

responsible for:

> ...approximately 57,000 active duty, Reserve and National Guard Soldiers, Sailors, Airmen, Marines and DoD civilians assigned to the headquarters, its four components and one sub-unified command. USSOCOM's components are U.S. Army Special Operations Command (USASOC), Naval Special Warfare Command (NAVSPECWARCOM), Air Force Special Operations Command (AFSOC) and Marine Corps Forces Special Operations Command (MARSOC). The Joint Special Operations Command (JSOC) is a USSOCOM sub-unified command.[4]

Further, USSOCOM develops special operations strategy, doctrine and tactics and as directed by the Unified Command Plan, USSOCOM is responsible for synchronizing Department of Defense (DoD) plans against global terrorist networks and receives, reviews, coordinates and prioritizes all DoD plans that support the global campaign against terror. Amongst special operation forces core activities are Counterterrorism and Counterinsurgency operations.[5]

> To further common understanding, Joint Publication 1-02 defines:
> - *Terrorism* as, "The unlawful use of violence or threat of violence to instill fear and coerce governments or societies. Terrorism is often motivated by religious, political, or other ideological beliefs and committed in the pursuit of goals that are usually political."[6]
>
> - *Counterterrorism* (CT) as, "Actions taken directly against terrorist networks and indirectly to influence and render global and regional environments inhospitable to terrorist networks." [7]
>
> - *Counterinsurgency* (COIN) as, "Comprehensive civilian and military efforts taken to defeat an insurgency and to address any core grievances."[8]
>
> - *Irregular Warfare* (IW) as, "A violent struggle among state and non-state actors for legitimacy and influence over the relevant populations(s). Irregular warfare favors indirect and asymmetric approaches, though it may employ thee full range of military and other capacities, in order to erode an adversary's power, influence, and will.[9]

Terrorism and CT as defined by Joint Publication 1-02, allow very local entities to be

classified as terrorists and possibly requiring attention from a CT force. Conversely, a

decade of conflict lent experiences to the US government and US military that have

been used to inform US national security strategy documents and joint doctrine development and updates e.g. 2006 Quadrennial Defense Review; National Security Strategy ((NSS) May 2010); National Defense Strategy ((NDS) June 2008); National Military Strategy ((NMS) 2011); National Strategy for Counterterrorism ((NSCT) June 2011); Quadrennial Roles and Missions Report (January 2009); Capstone Concept for Joint Operations version 3 (January 2009); Irregular Warfare: Countering Irregular Threats Joint Operating Concept version 2 ((IWJOC) May 2010); Department of Defense Directive 3000.07 – Irregular Warfare (December 2008); Joint Publication 3-24, Counterinsurgency Operations (October 2009); and Joint Publication 3-26, Counterterrorism (November 2009). Strategy and doctrine documents are updated, some mandated by law, others as lessons and understanding increase and demand updates or clarification. The US national security apparatus has acknowledged CT forces, special operation forces, *and* conventional forces have a role in irregular warfare of which CT is one of five principle activities. CT operations are no longer an exclusive domain for a single national CT force but also a requirement for special operations forces and conventional forces.[10]

Irregular Warfare

Irregular threats are adaptive state or non-state adversaries such as terrorists, insurgents, and criminal networks that resort to irregular forms of warfare to challenge conventional military powers. As articulated in the Irregular Warfare Joint Operating Concept (IW JOC), the US Joint Force approach to countering irregular threats is to prevent, deter, disrupt, and defeat irregular threats, with prevention being the primary focus of the effort. The IW JOC identifies five principle activities or operations that are undertaken in sequence, parallel, or in a blended form to coherently address irregular threats: counterterrorism (CT), unconventional warfare (UW), foreign internal defense (FID), counterinsurgency (COIN), and stability operations (SO).[11]

The previously listed strategy and doctrine documents are clear about the need for a whole-of-government approach, integration of all elements of national power, interagency inclusiveness, collaboration with partners of many types, and unifying efforts to deal with irregular threats and to counter terrorism.[12] The NDS states, "We will continue to work to improve understanding and harmonize best practices amongst interagency partners. This must happen at every level from Washington, DC-based headquarters to the field."[13] There seems to be wide recognition and acknowledgement that each element relies on the other to accomplish varied missions and that there are no independent actors achieving national objectives in isolation.[14] Directives to coordinate, cooperate, complement and integrate efforts permeate the national strategy documents.[15] However, there is an obvious absence of directives or inferences for the military services to work together, which leads to the assumption that the President, Secretary of Defense, and Chairman of the Joint Chiefs of Staff understand US military forces are inextricably integrated – "joint" – and the focus of strategic documents has shifted to discussing the "whole of government" or "whole of nation" approach which demands greater interagency and greater multinational cooperation (many references to partners, allies, and coalitions are included in the strategy documents).[16]

If the assumption the US military is joint holds, a subset of the joint force – the CT force – should be examined. The SOCOM CT force is a joint force that routinely operates as a joint special operations task force; however, although joint, the CT force has an impressive history of excelling as an insular force. Only recently did the CT force recognize the need to be more transparent and be an overt team member if it was to gain, maintain, and even increase the force's freedom of action throughout COIN operating environments. Specific CT force commanders and interagency leaders were key to increasing transparency and team play of their respective insular organizations.[17]

One of the first culture changes occurred within the CT force where historically stove piped and competitive units were directed to complement (and perhaps compliment) the others efforts. War facilitated this directive as for the first time in its history, the CT force had more requirements than it had forces to address the requirements. The competition to *get into the fight* dissipated and the command sought to maximize CT force efficiency and effectiveness as requirements for effects quickly outstripped CT force capacity. Internally, the insular CT force noted the expanded effects achieved when all CT force units sought complementary effects. The CT force quickly achieved maximum efficiency and effectiveness and then the CT force focused externally to increase the size, competency (speed), and effects of the entire CT team. Increasing the team size required diplomacy and sincerity to waylay concerns of the insular internal team members and to attract skeptical external members to the newly constructed "big tent."[18]

The CT force did not waver from offering greater transparency in an effort to gain increased trust, efficiency, and battlefield effects. Complementary personalities and war time resources allowed organizations that historically shared the minimum information required and pursued organizational ends, sometimes to the detriment of national objectives, to proactively complement the others efforts.[19] Transparency increased dramatically through a decade of war, in two theaters, as the CT force sought to build a network that could beat the insurgents' networks. The CT force anticipated and quickly noted the synergy attained by allowing more players onto the team; CT force effects increased exponentially. These efforts are accurately captured in General Stanley A. McChrystal's article, *It Takes a Network*[20] and Eric Schmitt and Thom Shanker's book, *Counterstrike: The Untold Story of America's Secret Campaign Against Al Qaeda.*[21]

The CT force created a network of unprecedented effectiveness. It simultaneously operated in multiple theaters and achieved unequalled successes in each. The CT force increased its tools and forces and continuously improved its tactics, techniques, and procedures (TTP). The CT force was a learning organization that prided itself on its disciplined and extensive after action review procedures that not only cataloged lessons from each operation but disseminated, incorporated, and thus continuously bettered itself through critical review. Classified statistics tell a story of steadily increasing effectiveness by all metrics.

Despite its comparatively light footprint and a restrictive mandate, the CT force's numerous unheralded successes directly contributed to unhinging Al Qaeda from Afghanistan and the initial defeat of the Taliban.[22] Then in early 2003, Iraq became the CT force's main effort and Afghanistan transitioned to a supporting or secondary effort. The CT force's size, responsibilities, and effects expanded in the Iraqi theater far beyond their previous capabilities.[23] The learned CT force defeated Al Qaeda in Iraq, where it dramatically contributed to conventional force successes as well.[24]

It was in Iraq that the CT force became a catalyst for unprecedented interagency cooperation and inter-service coordination.[25] The CT force was, and remains, secretive out of necessity. Yet its need to protect information does not detract from the value of its hard-earned lessons as CT force lessons are routinely shared throughout the services in order to better the overall operation of the United States Military. Aspects of its increased transparency and cooperation with conventional forces conducting Counterinsurgency Operations (COIN) played an integral role in the military's overall organizational growth.[26] The evolution of CT forces' methods of operation – TTPs – drove its success. Its targeting process – known as Find, Fix, Finish, Exploit, and Analyze (or F3EA) – was continuously refined. New technologies and additional resources, including enhanced communication, Intelligence, Surveillance and Reconnaissance (ISR), analytical tools and analysts, enhanced the F3EA process.[27] Information sharing within the military – between the CT forces and conventional forces – increased, and conventional force assets and capabilities were brought to bear on the problem sets and targets facing the CT force.[28] In short, greater cooperation yielded more effective battlefield results. The process demonstrated that complementing operations were better than unilateral operations conducted by CT or conventional forces.[29]

Iraq remained the CT force's main effort until 2010, when the CT force realigned and Afghanistan again emerged as the main effort with Iraq devolving to a secondary effort. In Afghanistan, the CT force and interagency coordination once again evolved significantly. At the direction of the CT force commander, unprecedented transparency was availed to the conventional forces, known as the Battle Space Owners (BSOs) – the forces that conduct Counterinsurgency Operations (COIN) and are responsible for holding and operating in a set geographic area. The CT force addressed the BSO concerns and target sets, and shared intelligence, exploitation, and assets. The BSO provided much needed conventional support and human intelligence, which required local familiarity. Transparency and coordinated efforts between the CT and COIN forces led to complementary effects and unprecedented freedom of action for the CT force. The realignment, evolution, transparency, coordinated efforts, complementary effects, and unprecedented freedom of action were driven by a series of CT force commanders that understood calculated transparency yields unprecedented battlefield effects.[30]

Irregular Warfare – Afghanistan

The CT force was a team building organization with recent team building successes. The CT force broke down internal barriers to better CT force effects.[31] The CT force proactively brought supporting agencies onto the team and into the tent where complementary and synergistic effects were realized.[32] But the CT force initially struggled to expand the team concept to the conventional forces (CF) or general purpose forces (GPF); this was especially so in Afghanistan. The CF or GPF – throughout the Coalition – are routinely referred to as battle space owners (BSO) in a COIN operating environment.

The Afghan theater illustrates the complexity of CT force and BSO relations and illuminates the CT force efforts to increase transparency and ultimately increase effects. In Afghanistan, the BSO conducts full-spectrum COIN operations. Full-spectrum COIN operations require the BSO to live and work amongst the population and nearly without fail be partnered with Afghan National Security Forces (ANSF). Living amongst the population, perhaps with ANSF, and operating with ANSF amongst the population, allows the BSO to "feel" the operating environment in a different way than a raiding force. Increased transparency increased effects of the CT force and the BSO, which increased freedom of action for both the CT force and BSO further increasing Coalition effects throughout the theater. The road to complementary effects was not fast or without bumps but once directed by the CT commander, the CT force embraced the directive and sought to develop and disseminate TTPs that maximized each force's strengths.

In early 2009, General McChrystal's successor, who maintained continuity of thought and action, believed networks defeated networks and team play was integral to strengthening networks. Although Iraq was the CT force main effort it was apparent the main effort would switch to Afghanistan in the near future. The CT force commander became increasingly focused on Afghanistan as he sought to set conditions for realigning his main effort. Although the CT force had been operating in Afghanistan for eight years, the CT force commander noted that, for a period of time, some BSOs did more to stymie the CT force's freedom of action than did the enemy or the Afghan military or government. A series of events led to a tactical pause and wholesale reevaluation of CT efforts and strategy in Afghanistan. The reevaluation showed a lack of transparency with the BSO was a corrosive issue that directly affected CT force freedom of action. The CT force commander directed planners to review targeting, BSO coordination, information operations and anything else deemed relevant to maintaining then increasing CT force freedom of action.[33]

The CT force joint planning group (JPG) recommended changes to the CT forces targeting methodology, which directly related to BSO coordination and to information operations. The recommendations were evolutionary and focused on (counter-culture) transparency – highlighting not all CT force information was secret or top secret and that sharing information would lead to BSO buy in and support in heretofore unrealized ways. It was noted that many in the CT force served in conventional force units throughout their careers – attending pre-commissioning training, professional military education courses, and special skill schools together over a period of decades. The relationships built over decades were an immense strength to bring into the network but until 2009, the personal relationships between the CT force and BSOs in Afghanistan were rarely exploited for continual mutual benefit.

The CT force strategy was approved in late winter 2009 and a proof of principle was conducted in spring of 2009. CT force elements partnered with a BSO that had recently left the CT force for conventional force battalion command (in Afghanistan). The personalities were right to develop and share TTPs that would allow the CT force to quickly pass intelligence, targets, and assets to the BSO and for the BSO to quickly pass information to the CT force. In short order, the synergistic effect of the BSO having access to the CT force intelligence and assets and the CT force having access to the knowledge only a population-centric BSO can gather was a model to be replicated. In addition to F3EA targeting, the CT force was able to leverage the network to produce exceptionally accurate, relevant, and timely information operation (IO) products that were shared with the BSOs from battalion to International Security Assistance Force (ISAF) level. The IO efforts – non-lethal effects – were continuous in the population-centric COIN environment of Afghanistan. The non-lethal effects shaped the environment by providing timely and accurate information to the BSO, Afghan partners, and the Afghan population.

After the proof of principle the CT force, in coordination with ISAF, disseminated the TTPs and effects to all BSOs. As one example of the synergy attained, in the summer of 2009, a CT element was committed to a BSO area that had experienced nineteen US casualties to IEDs in a period of three days. In 30 days of synchronized operations, the CT element helped reduce IED events by 90%, which dramatically increased the BSO freedom of action and thus ability to conduct more effective population-centric COIN operations.[34]

In summer 2009, the ISAF Commander visited the CT force and sought a briefing on the CT force strategy. In the brief the ISAF Commander, who knew the CT force exceptionally well, asked, how the CT force measures effectiveness? A CT force commander replied, "the same way I measured effectiveness when I served as a BSO – freedom of action."[35] Acknowledging the CT force had the assets to ensure freedom of action anywhere, the truer test in a COIN environment was to assess Coalition Force, Afghan Security Force, Afghan Government, population, and NGO freedom of action. The ISAF Commander accepted that answer but immediately followed up with, how does the CT force (a national asset) ensure it is being decisive? The same commander, stated the CT force was not decisive in the Afghanistan COIN environment but what the CT force did was create white space for the BSOs to conduct COIN operations which have a cumulative (v. decisive) effect over time.[36]

The CT force continued to evolve and mature. Although the CT force had only a coordinating relationship with the ISAF Commander, the CT force commander made it well known that the CT force was a supporting effort to the ISAF commander and the BSOs. He famously and routinely stated, "we'll do windows if that is what it takes to

11

maintain our freedom of action."[37] The overt display of mutual respect for and support of the BSOs dramatically increased the CT force freedom of action. Statistically, the CT force was more precise than any force in the history of warfare but that did not preclude all civilian deaths or the accusation of civilian deaths. At these unfortunate times, the support of the BSO, Afghan Security Forces, Afghan Government, and population was essential to maintaining CT force freedom of action. When regrettable events occurred, the default setting of the BSO and those Afghans that interacted with the BSO was not accusatory towards the CT force but instead it was acknowledged that bad things happen to good people and good units and unfortunately some innocents are hurt in war. Actions were immediately taken by the BSO – and supported by the CT force – to culturally address the misstep or perceived misstep. Support provided to the CT force was garnered through relationships that were built on transparency and humility.

The CT force commander, drawing on lessons from Iraq, knew the CT force in Afghanistan needed Afghan partners. To the surprise of many, he quickly retained Afghan senior partners from the ministry of defense, ministry of interior and Afghan intelligence community and he directed they be allowed to operate within the guarded CT force camp. The senior partners operated adjacent to the CT joint operations center (JOC) on a 24 hour schedule as they monitored all missions from the summer 2009 forward. Shortly thereafter, the CT force sought like Afghan partners at tactical unit (or strike force) level, the CT force embarked on one of the most successful efforts to create a professional and credible partnered force that has been on nearly every objective since 2010.[38] When it was suggested that females be included with the strike forces to more properly address Afghan females on objectives, the CT force embraced the idea and sought US Army Special Operations Command's assistance in developing what became known as Cultural Support Teams.[39] In comparatively short order, well trained US military females were on objectives with the strike forces in order to properly address Afghan culture and concerns.

The CT force is the nation's most resourced military force. Its strength is its people. Over time, "its people" included a network of people from the interagency to the most conventional BSO, to include Coalition BSOs.[40] The CT force benefitted from transparency as the conventional forces augmented the CT force with aircraft and surveillance platforms – increasing the CT force capabilities and freedom of action – which in turn allowed more strike forces to precisely action more targets in the BSO area of operations.

There are times and places for the CT force to be and remain very secretive. But as the US strategy and doctrine leans towards irregular warfare – CT, UW, FID, COIN, SO – future battle spaces are likely to be shared. The lessons from Iraq and even more so from Afghanistan show transparency, where possible, creates synergistic effects between the CT force and conventional forces leading to greater effects for all. Although the following lessons were gleaned in COIN environments, many of the lessons are likely applicable to the other irregular warfare environments.

Lessons Gleaned from a Decade of War:

- Each operating environment is complex and unique. If CT force operations are conducted in the environment they may precede or follow a myriad of special operation force or conventional force efforts. It is very likely, like in the two recent operations (Operation Enduring Freedom – Afghanistan and Operation Iraqi Freedom), that CT force operations will precede, overlap, *and* follow conventional force efforts.[41] As the operating environment matures or changes so must CT force operations. With few in the operating environment, CT forces have more latitude or freedom of action. As more players – special forces, conventional forces, multinational forces, United Nations forces, interagency and others – populate the operating environment, there is an expectation that coordination, cooperation, and ideally complementary and integrated effects will be realized. The first force to detect the changes in the environment seems obligated to proactively seek to coordinate (v. ignore) with others in an effort to mitigate what may evolve into complicating and distracting issues.

- Personalities matter – if the first CT personality or first BSO personality is not ripe to the idea of transparency and increased effects, seek another personality. Little effort invested will produce the personality that shares common history and common desire to strengthen the team and improve the network.

- Timings matter – as discussed earlier, CT forces may precede, overlap, or follow conventional forces. When CT forces are committed, there is likely a threat that requires their attention for some period. The CT force has learned the value of liaison officers (LNO) out to Brigade Combat Team, Regional Command, Joint Command, and Theater Command level. The CT force also understands the need to take in LNOs. BSOs at all levels should be proactive at engaging the CT force *in their battle space* and seeking a CT force LNO as well as offering an LNO to the CT force. LNO personalities matter and the CT force is committed to providing the best personality to the task, whether that be a sergeant, lieutenant, captain, major, or colonel. A common phrase in the CT force is, "if your LNOs out don't hurt, you likely sent the wrong person." Quality investments pay quality dividends.

- COIN environments require all forces to work with elements of the host nation amongst the population. Leveraging the BSO is a means to gain rapid understanding of the population and a means to mitigate issues within the BSO's area of operation. The CT force brings incredible resources and precision to an imprecise operating environment. Leveraging the CT force – which may mean providing the CT force scarce resources such as aircraft, surveillance platforms, or partners – is sure to pay dividends that exceed initial expectations.

- Senior-level and credible host nation partners in the construct of a coordination or advisory group – treated as true partners – coupled with well trained and disciplined host nation partners at the tactical level (level that interfaces with the population) increase freedom of action for conventional forces as well as the CT force. Building these [credible] capabilities requires commander direction and involvement and a credible and quality investment in resources. Authorities associated with host nation entities must be understood and leveraged i.e. the Afghan National Army, like the US Army, has restrictions on entering homes and on arresting Afghan citizens; the Afghan National Police have arrest and search authorities; the Afghan Border

Police have search and arrest authorities within 50 kilometers of the border. The investment in host nation partners pay dividends in freedom of action.

- Partners, at every level, should improve in competence and confidence on a daily basis. Additionally, coalition force understanding of and confidence in the partners should improve daily. This only occurs if credible and continuous investment is made in the partners and the relationships. At the tactical level, partners must be trained (on common equipment, maintenance, and TTPs to include insertion and extraction techniques), equipped, [fully] integrated, routinely show cased to host nation and coalition leaders, and held accountable. Coalition understanding of host nation culture must improve daily; this is important in countless ways but particularly in reference to religion, diet, family, pass and leaves, medical treatment, handling of remains in accordance with religious customs, and respect. The application of the "Golden Rule" – in absence of particular knowledge, treat others as one would wish their parents or grandparents be treated – alleviates issues associated with cultural ignorance.

- Cultural Support Team-like entities were slow to evolve but once developed and incorporated alleviated concerns and complaints about a number of cultural sensitivities – protecting or increasing freedom of action. The unanticipated benefits of the interaction of US females with host nation females and adolescents were extensive but do not warrant elaboration in this form.

- The CT force is composed of our nation's most highly trained and best equipped service members. Each is prepared to routinely risk his or her life to protect American citizens, allies, and partners. Occasionally, the CT force may need to be reminded that service members living in an irregular warfare environment likely fall into one of the above categories – citizen, ally, or partner – and it is as honorable to protect other service members as it is to protect non-service members from hazards such as internal threats, enemy IED or IDF networks, and enemy C2. Conversely, the operative word in battle space owner is "owner" and BSOs should own and control their battle space and not rely on others – the CT force – to address routine threats in their battle space.

- The CT force F3EA targeting process is well known to many in the conventional force. F3EA was written about in professional journals and discussed as a TTP in a number of Army professional schools.[42] The CT force has the most highly trained subject matter experts in the world that can be leveraged by the BSO for all aspects of the F3EA targeting process. Many targets do not require the CT force but are better executed – with reduced risk to mission, force, and population – with CT force enablers (people or other assets). The CT force is more likely to pass targets and assets to BSOs that are willing and able to execute targets than one might expect. The trust associated with passing targets and assets is cumulative and built over time. Engagement at LNO and commander level will facilitate F3EA-type conversations that should include discussing CT force and BSO authorities for action.

- New technologies and additional resources, including enhanced communication, Intelligence, Surveillance and Reconnaissance (ISR), analytical tools and analysts, have enhanced the F3EA targeting process.[43] Information sharing within the military – between the CT forces and conventional forces – has increased and CT force and conventional force assets and capabilities are routinely brought to bear on the problem sets and targets facing one force or the other. In short, greater cooperation yields more effective battlefield results. The process consistently demonstrates that complementing operations are better than unilateral operations conducted by CT or conventional forces and it is up to all team members to seek (and provide) the greatest effects possible.[44]

- The F3EA targeting process puts a premium on exploitation and analysis.[45] The CT force has unparalleled means to exploit and analyze but at times conditions may prevent the CT force from immediately securing and exploiting a target. The BSO may get offered CT force ISR, lift, and fires assets or conditions may be such that the CT force is asking for BSO assets to secure a specific target in the BSO's area of operation. BSOs that are able and willing to secure and or exploit CT force targets – and possibly share assets – will build trust, respect, and encourage future cooperation that is likely to pay dividends to both forces.

- In a COIN environment, trust is put to the test when there is an issue that requires mitigation. Trust between the BSO and his host nation partners, trust between the CT force and BSO, trust between BSO and their chain of command, and trust between the CT force and their chain of command as well as the partners they coordinate with. BSOs know the personalities in their area of operations and many in their area of interest. BSOs generally develop relations that can be leveraged to mitigate a wide array of issues that arise in complex COIN environments. When issues arise that require mitigation, the BSO must be willing to quickly take on the mitigating role – even at high cost – and the CT force must be fast, accurate, and supportive when reporting to the BSO. Failing to fully disclose information at any juncture can fracture trust and relations across the network. BSOs will be more likely to assist the CT force that establishes relations prior to mitigation being required.

- In the recent extended conflicts, the CT force has been continuously deployed since 2001. The information about the operating environment that resides within the CT force is unparalleled. BSOs can seek to take advantage of this information at home station, at the numerous CT force CONUS hubs, or when arriving in theater. In Afghanistan, the CT force has been exceptional at reaching out to incoming BSOs – in future environments, BSOs may have to reach out to the CT force until relations are reestablished.

Conclusion

Although Iraq and Afghanistan are very different theaters, lessons shared between them opened doors for cooperative initiatives and organizational growth. Iraq was a nearly ideal operational environment with comparatively developed infrastructure, benign terrain, adequately enabled conventional forces, a more exploitable target set, and a very different detention apparatus that housed a culturally different type of detainee. These factors led to a more effective and efficient F3EA targeting process. Afghanistan is on the other end of the spectrum – geographically larger and faced with extreme terrain, limited and under-developed infrastructure, weather challenges, sanctuary that is exploited, a larger fragmented population and target set, limited detention capacity, and lower density of US troops. These differences make it particularly remarkable that the lessons of CT, Interagency, and conventional coordination could be shared across theaters. The combination of lessons from Iraq and 10 years of operating in Afghanistan yields a more capable and efficient CT force moving into a new phase of US military engagement – Irregular Warfare.[46]

The actions of a few insightful leaders may have served as a catalyst to focus strategic guidance on the need for better coordination, cooperation, and complementary effects and these same leaders may have served as a catalyst to implement (and rewrite) joint doctrine as they matured CT force and interagency efforts from conflicting efforts, through deconflicted efforts, through coordinated efforts, to cooperative, and onto complementary and integrated efforts. Getting to complementary and integrated efforts required culture changes within many organizations and agencies. Leaders and commanders with the vision to evolve and better their unprecedented battlefield effects set the tone for all to be better team members and in many cases team leaders, to trade arrogance for humility, and trade insular notions for inclusive actions, which all resulted in a joint force of unmatched capability.

The past decade's successes in balancing the necessity of protecting secrets with the need to enable sufficient transparency and share lessons have created more capable team members and partners and should serve as a standard to maintain and build upon.[47] As forces and agencies redeploy, budgets constrict, and mission sets evolve, leadership across the network will be required to maintain and strengthen the networks of networks and enlighten or marginalize biased or corrosive personalities that threaten complementary and integrated effects and thus freedom of action.

Endnotes

[1]"3rd Ranger Battalion: Battle Tested, Combat Proven," linked from The 75th Ranger Regiment 'Go Army' Home Page at "Heritage," http://www.goarmy.com/ranger/heritage/third-ranger-battalion.html (accessed November 11, 2011).

[2]"History: United States Special Operations Command," March 31, 2008, linked from the USSOCOM Home Page at http://www.socom.mil/Documents/history6thedition.pdf (accessed November 11, 2011).

[3]Eric Schmitt and Thom Shanker, *Counterstrike: The Untold Story of America's Secret Campaign Against Al Qaeda*, (New York, Times Books – Henry Holt and Company, 2011), 83, 91-2.

[4]"About SOCOM: United States Special Operations Command," linked from the USSOCM home page at http://www.socom.mil/Pages/AboutUSSOCOM.aspx (accessed February 2, 2012).

[5]Ibid.

[6]U.S. Joint Chiefs of Staff, *Department of Defense Dictionary of Military and Associated Terms*, Joint Publication 1-02 (Washington, DC: U.S. Joint Chiefs of Staff, November 8, 2010 (as amended through January 15, 2012)), 336.

[7]Ibid., 78.

[8]Ibid., 77.

[9]Ibid., 172.

[10]U.S. Joint Chiefs of Staff, *Counterterrorism,* Joint Publication 3-26 (Washington, DC: U.S. Joint Chiefs of Staff, November 13, 2009), XVI.

[11]Michael G. Mullen, *Irregular Warfare: Countering Irregular Threats Joint Operating Concept Version 2.0* (Washington: DC: The Pentagon, May 17, 2010), 4-5.

[12]Barack H. Obama, *National Security Strategy* (Washington, DC: The White House, May 2010), 14; Barack H. Obama, *National Security Strategy for Counterterrorism* (Washington, DC: The White House, June 2011), 2 and 7.

[13]Robert M. Gates, *National Defense Strategy,* (Washington, DC: The Pentagon, June 2008), 18.

[14]Ibid., 19.

[15]Obama, *National Security* Strategy, 14; Obama, *National Security Strategy for Counterterrorism*, 2 and 7.

[16]Gates, *National Defense Strategy*, 1, 8, 15, and 17; Obama, *National Security Strategy for Counterterrorism,* 2 and 7.

[17]Stanley A. McChrystal, "It Takes a Network," March/April 2011, http://www.foreignpolicy.com/articles/2011/02/22/it_takes_a_network?print=yes&hidecomments=yes&page=full (accessed November 12, 2011).

[18]Ibid.

[19]Ibid.

[20]Ibid.

[21]Schmitt, *"Counterstrike"*, 91-2, 98.

[22]Steve Bowman and Catherine Dale, "War in Afghanistan: Strategy, Military Operations, and Issues for Congress," December 3, 2009, http://www.fas.org/sgp/crs/row/R40156.pdf (accessed November 12, 2011). "Military victory, including the demise of the Taliban regime, came quickly. In November 2001, the Taliban fled Kabul, and in December they left their stronghold, the southern city of Kandahar. It is generally understood that in December 2001, key al Qaeda and Taliban leaders fled across the border into Pakistan."

[23]McChrystal, "It Takes a Network."

[24]Anthony H. Cordesman, "Victory and Violence in Iraq: Reducing the Irreducible Minimum," http://csis.org/files/media/csis/pubs/080227_irreducible.minimum.final.pdf (accessed November 12, 2011). "More quietly, the US was able to combine major improvements in its intelligence, surveillance,

and reconnaissance capabilities with greatly improved Iraqi human intelligence. It was able to target much of the AQI network and key Shi'ite extremists, and use precision air strikes, carefully planned raids, and air mobility to be far more effective in decapitating the leaders of the insurgency."

[25]Schmitt, "*Counterstrike*," 91-2.

[26]Thom Shanker, "Admiral Defends Use of Elite Unit in Calamitous Raid," August 30, 2011, linked from the *New York Times Home Page* at World / Asia Pacific at http://www.nytimes.com/2011/08/31/world/asia/31commander.html (accessed November 12, 2011). "Admiral McRaven dismissed assertions that the most highly trained Navy and Army commando teams should be reserved solely for the most high-profile missions; he said they were regularly assigned to support commanders of units in a local area of combat if that contributed to the overall mission." "We have to be fungible as a force," Admiral McRaven said. "And if we are not fungible as a force, then we are not of value. It is not unusual at all for Seals or Rangers or Army Special Operations forces to be part of a quick-reaction force, as in this case."

[27]McChrystal, "It Takes a Network."

[28]Schmitt, "*Counterstrike*," 75.

[29]Ibid.

[30]Stanley A. McChrystal and Tom Brokaw, "HBO History Makers Series with Stanley McChrystal (Transcript)," October 6, 2011, linked from the Council on Foreign Relations home page at "Publications (CFR Events)," http://www.cfr.org/afghanistan/hbo-history-makers-series-stanley-mcchrystal/p26157 (accessed November 12, 2011). "You know, there's a dichotomy that's drawn sometimes between COIN and counterterrorist operations. And I think it's absolutely a false one, at least it's false in the way people do it. If I say counterterrorist operations to most people, they think that's direct action. That's either a kinetic strike or a raid by a force. And if we talk about counterinsurgency, we tend to think of hearts and minds. In fact, direct action is part of counterinsurgency, just as reducing the causes is part of counterterrorism. So I'll talk about direct action as opposed to CT." "Dave Petraeus says it better than I ever will. You're never going to kill your way to victory or capture. What you are going to do is help reduce the enemy threat while you reduce the causes of the problem. Even terrorism is that way."

[31]Schmitt, "*Counterstrike*," 83.

[32]McChrystal, "It Takes a Network"

[33]Interview with confidential source September 27, 2011; CT force commanders/leaders will not be identified in unclassified publications.

[34]Ibid.

[35]Ibid.

[36]Ibid.

[37]Interview with confidential source September 28, 2011; CT force commanders will not be identified in unclassified publications.

[38]Austin Long, "Partners or Proxies? U.S. Host Nation Cooperation in Counterterrorism Operations," CTC Sentinel Online 4, 11-2, (November 2011): 13, http://www.ctc.usma.edu/wp-content/uploads/2011/12/CTCSentinel-Vol4Iss11-124.pdf (accessed February 23, 2012).

[39]"About the Cultural Support Program: United States Army Special Operations Command John F. Kennedy Special Warfare Center and School," linked from the USASOC home page at http://www.soc.mil/swcs/cst/about.html (accessed February 17, 2012).

[40]McChrystal, "It Takes a Network."

[41]Mullen, *Irregular Warfare,* 22.

[42]Michael T. Flynn, Rich Juergens,a nd Thomas L. Cantrell, "Employing ISR: SOF Best Practices," Joint Forces Quarterly Online 50, (3rd quarter 2008): 57, http://www.dtic.mil/cgi-bin/GetTRDoc?AD=ADA516799 (accessed January 20, 2012).

[43]Ibid.

[44]Ibid.

[45]Ibid.

[46]McChrysal, "It Takes a Network," "From its birth in Iraq, both the actual network -- and the hard-earned appreciation for that organizational model -- increasingly expanded to Afghanistan, especially as our nation's focus turned toward that theater;" William H. McRaven, "Future of U.S. Special Operations Forces: Ten Years After 9/11 and Twenty-Five Years After Goldwater-Nichols," Congressional Record (September 22, 2011): http://armedservices.house.gov/index.cfm/files/serve?File_id=2d29a1f6-b1f2-4ee1-808f-d51a8322bafc. "First, we will continue to lead and deliver the nation's premier CT fighting force. Simultaneously we must also provide, with Service enablers, the preponderance of forces for sustained counterinsurgency and stability operations globally. This combined mission is currently seen in the simultaneous SOF leadership and tacit execution of the CT and Village Stability Operations in Afghanistan. As a result of these unique enduring SOF requirements, the projected conventional force drawdown in Afghanistan through 2014 is increasingly dependent upon significant SOF presence. Conventional force reductions will not equate to comparable reductions in SOF. But, when fully integrated within a comprehensive whole-of-government approach, the breadth of capability displayed in this current campaign provides the clearest evidence of SOF's inherent flexibility, agility, and value in addressing irregular missions. One of the explicit lessons of the last decade of conflict is the absolute necessity to share information, plan, and operate in concert with our interagency and foreign partners. Born of our extensive presence and cultivated relationships, SOF has uniquely embraced this approach."

[47]McRaven, "Future of U.S. Special Operations Forces: Ten Years After 9/11 and Twenty-Five Years After Goldwater-Nichols."